THE
Language
OF
Description

AN ONLINE SELLER'S
WORD REFERENCE GUIDE

Ellen Beeler
Visuaria Publishing • 2012

The Language of Description: An Online Seller's Word
Reference Guide

© 2012 Visuaria Publishing

ISBN print edition: 978-0-9841757-5-8

CONTENTS

introduction

Write Better Descriptions!

You have some wonderful items for sale in your online venue. You are getting some views and you want people to love your items as much as you do. Don't sabotage your sales with boring or incomplete product descriptions that use the same old over-used words! Buyers need to see, feel, imagine, touch, and taste the beauty and perfection of the item to feel good about making a purchase. You need to not only describe the features and benefits of your item, to paint a picture with words, but also to help your customers imagine how it will integrate into their lives, how they will feel when it belongs to them.

You know that your descriptions should be longer and more interesting and lively and, well, more descriptive. But what if you sit down to write them and find yourself at a loss for words? Even if you have excellent writing skills, it can be very difficult to accurately describe and sing the praises of your own finds or creations.

This guide is intended to serve as a quick resource for finding the right words to make your descriptions pop and eloquently convey the true qualities and benefits of your creations or finds. Having a "word bank" at your fingertips can help you convey more thorough and accurate information, capture the buyer's interest, tell your story, and make a compelling case for purchase.

Of course these lists could never be comprehensive, and the language of description is very subjective, but they will serve as an excellent collection that you can add to, research, and return to again and again for inspiration.

What Does It Look Like?

Words that describe size, dimension, or quantity

abundant	fitted	measure
ample	fits easily	measurement
average	generous	medium
baggy	gigantic	micro
big	grand	mini
bountiful	handful	miniature
brief	hefty	multitude
broad	huge	oversized
bulky	immense	packed
chunky	jumbo	pair
collection	king-size	petite
colossal	large	plentiful
compact	larger than life	plump
copious	lavish	plus size
deep	length	pocket-sized
delicate	life-size	proportion
dense	little	quartet
diameter	long	queen-size
diminutive	loose	scaled-down
duo	lot	ratio
enormous	macro	reduced
expansive	mammoth	roomy
extra	massive	set
extra large	maxi	shallow
extra small	maximum	short

continued on next page

Words that describe size, dimension, or quantity

CONTINUED FROM PREVIOUS PAGE

sizable	streamlined	tiny
slender	substantial	titanic
slim	svelte	tremendous
small	tailored	trio
snug	tall	voluminous
space saving	thick	voluptuous
spacious	thin	wafer thin
statuesque	tight	wide

Words that describe weight

airy	featherweight	lightweight
bulky	heavy	mass
dense	heft	massive
featherlight	light	weightless

Words that describe shape or form

alignment	ergonomic	rounded
angled	figure	serpentine
angular	flat	shallow
arc	foreground	shapely
architecture	geometrical	short
arrangement	harmonious	slanted
asymmetrical	horizontal	solid
background	hourglass	spherical
balanced	irregular	spiral
branching	linear	square
circular	long	strand
concave	mold	streamlined
configuration	morph	structure
conical	narrow	sturdy
contour	oblique	symmetrical
contoured	oblong	tapering
convex	octagonal	three-dimen-
crescent	orb	sional
cubic	outline	tower
curvaceous	oval	trapezoid
curved	parallel	tubular
cut	pentagon	twist
cylindrical	perpendicular	uniform
diagonal	profile	vertical
diamond	proportioned	wedge
distributed	ratio	wide
dome	rectangular	
elliptical	rotund	

Words for colors

alabaster	canary yellow	emerald green
amber	candy apple red	flax
amethyst	carmine red	fluorescent
antique white	carnation pink	forest green
apricot	celadon	French blue
aquamarine	cerise	fuchsia
army green	cerulean	ginger
auburn	champagne	gold
avocado	charcoal	grape
azure	chartreuse	hot pink
baby blue	cherry	hunter green
banana	chocolate	indigo
battleship grey	cinnamon	ivory
beige	cobalt blue	jade
bisque	coffee	jet black
black	copper	kelly green
blond	coral	khaki
blush	coral pink	lavender
bone	cornflower blue	lemon
boysenberry	cream	lilac
brick red	crimson	lime
bronze	cyan	magenta
buff	earth	mahogany
burgundy	ebony	mango
burnt orange	ecru	maroon
burnt sienna	eggplant	mauve
burnt umber	electric blue	mint

Words for colors

CONTINUED FROM PREVIOUS PAGE

mocha	pumpkin	spring green
moss green	raspberry	straw
multicolored	robin's egg blue	sunny
mustard	rose	tangerine
navy	royal blue	taupe
obsidian	rust	tawny
olive green	salmon	teal
onyx	sapphire	turquoise
pastel	scarlet	vanilla
peach	sea green	violet
pearl	sepia	wheat
periwinkle	silver	watermelon
pewter	sky blue	wine
platinum	slate grey	
plum	smoky	

Words that describe color, finish or appearance

aura
bright
brightness
brilliant
burnished
clean
clear
complexion
contrast
crystalline
dark
deep
diffused
dusky
effervescent
faceted
feature
fiery
flushed
focal point
gauzy
glassy
glimmering
glittering

glittery
glowing
gossamer
hue
illuminated
incandescent
iridescent
jewel-toned
look
luminescent
luminous
lustrous
metallic
misty
mosaic
mottled
muted
neon
opaque
overtones
pale
panorama
pastel
patina

pigment
polish
prismatic
profile
radiant
rainbow
reflective
richly hued
shade
sheer
shimmery
shiny
sparkling
sparkly
tinge
tint
tone
translucent
twinkle
undertones
variegated
vivid

Words that describe pattern or ornament

allover
alternating
Arabesque
argyle
Asian
asymmetrical
balanced
banded
basketweave
bordered
brocade
candy-striped
Celtic
checked
checkered
chevron
Chinese
clustered
coil
collage
complex
criss cross
crosshatching
damask
dappled
device
diagonal

diamond
dotted
Egyptian
feather
flecked
fleur de lis
foliage
floral
flourish
flowered
fluted
fret
frieze
geometric
gingham
Gothic
grained
Greek key
herringbone
hound's tooth
interlaced
interlocking
irregular
labyrinth
lattice
linear
lotus

Madras
marbled
Medieval
monochrome
Moorish
moire
mosaic
mottled
naturalistic
optical illusion
organic
paisley
patterned
pinstripe
plaid
polka dot
pop art
psychedelic
quatrefoil
radial
random
Renaissance
rhythmic
rosette
scalloped
scroll
serial

continued on next page

Words that describe pattern or ornament

CONTINUED FROM PREVIOUS PAGE

speckled	symmetrical	twisty
spiral	tactile	variegated
spotted	tapestry	veined
stars	tartan	vignette
stipple	tessellation	vine
striated	textured	wave
striped	tiered	whorled
stylized	trefoil	woven
swirls	tweed	zigzag

How Does it Feel?

Words that describe texture

airy	frilly	ruffled
bumpy	frizzy	sculptured
buttery	furry	sensual
caressing	fuzzy	shaggy
coarse	grainy	sharp
cool	hammered	sheer
cozy	hard	shiny
crinkled	leathery	silky
crisp	light	slick
cuddly	lush	smooth
delicate	matte	soft
dense	metallic	spongy
downy	patina	stamped
embossed	plush	supple
engraved	pointy	transparent
feathery	polished	velvety
firm	prickly	waxy
flexible	puffy	whisper soft
fluffy	rough	woolly

Describe It!

A long list of descriptive adjectives

abstract
abundant
accent
adaptable
adorable
adorned
affordable
alluring
alternative
amazing
amusing
angelic
appealing
architectural
aromatic
artisan
artful
artistic
artsy
attractive
authentic
awe-inspiring
awesome
bizarre
beachy

beautiful
beauty
becoming
bestselling
blended
bling
bold
botanical
breathtaking
calming
captivating
casual
celestial
charming
cheerful
chic
chunky
classic
classy
clean
clean-lined
clever
colorful
comfortable
comforting

comfy
comic
compelling
complementary
complete
complex
conceptual
consummate
contemplative
contemporary
contrasting
convenient
cool
coordinated
cosmopolitan
cozy
creative
cuddly
curious
curvaceous
cushy
custom
cute
dainty
dapper

continued on next page

A long list of descriptive adjectives

CONTINUED FROM PREVIOUS PAGE

daring
dark
darling
dashing
dazzling
decadent
deconstructed
decorative
delicate
delicious
delightful
deluxe
designer
different
dignified
distinctive
distinguished
diverse
divine
down-to-earth
dramatic
dreamy
durable
dynamic
earth-inspired
earthy
easy

eccentric
eclectic
edgy
efficient
elaborate
elegant
embellished
emotional
empowering
enchanting
energizing
engaging
enhanced
enjoyable
entertaining
enticing
essential
ethereal
evocative
excellent
exciting
exclusive
exhilarating
existential
exotic
expressive
exquisite

extraordinary
eye-catching
eye-pleasing
famous
fancy
fantastic
fantasy
fashionable
faux
favorite
feisty
feminine
festive
fetching
figurative
fine
finest
first class
first rate
flare
flashy
flattering
flawless
flirtatious
flirty
floral
flowery

A long list of descriptive adjectives

CONTINUED FROM PREVIOUS PAGE

flowing	gracious	indulgent
fluid	graphic	innovative
folksy	gratifying	inspirational
formal	great	inspired
fragrant	grotesque	inspiring
fresh	handsome	intense
friendly	handy	interactive
frisky	healing	intimate
full	healthy	intoxicating
fun	heavy duty	intricate
functional	hilarious	intrinsic
funkadelic	hip	intuitive
funky	historical	invaluable
funny	holistic	irrational
futuristic	homemade	irresistible
geeky	homey	jazzed-up
genteel	hot	jazzy
gentle	humorous	kid-friendly
genuine	hypnotic	kitschy
girly	iconic	lasting
glam	ideal	lavish
glamorous	imaginative	leisurely
glorious	impeccable	loose
goddess	important	lovely
good-looking	incomparable	low-key
gorgeous	incredible	luxe
graceful	indispensable	luxurious

continued on next page

A long list of descriptive adjectives

CONTINUED FROM PREVIOUS PAGE

magical	nerdy	portable
magnificent	noble	posh
manly	noir	powerful
marvelous	nostalgic	practical
masculine	novel	precious
masterful	open	precise
matching	optimal	preferred
mathematical	opulent	premium
meditative	organic	pretty
mesmerizing	original	priceless
mindblowing	ornamental	primary
minimalist	ornate	primitive
modest	outrageous	proven
modish	panache	pure
monumental	passionate	quality
motivational	peasant	quintessential
mouthwatering	perfect	quirky
moving	personal	radiant
multipurpose	personality-filled	radical
mysterious	phenomenal	rakish
mystical	picturesque	rare
natty	playful	red hot
natural	pleasing	refined
naturalistic	plush	refreshing
nature-inspired	poetic	regal
naughty	polished	reinforced
necessary	popular	relaxing

A long list of descriptive adjectives

CONTINUED FROM PREVIOUS PAGE

reliable	simple	sultry
remarkable	sleek	sumptuous
restrained	slinky	sunny
retro	snug	superb
rhythmic	sophisticated	superior
rich	snazzy	supreme
ritzy	soothing	surprising
robust	soulful	surreal
romantic	special	swanky
rugged	spectacular	sweet
rustic	spicy	swirling
sacred	splendid	symbolic
sassy	sporty	tailored
satisfying	spot-on	tantalizing
savory	state-of-the-art	tasteful
savvy	streamlined	tasty
scary	striking	terrific
seasoned	strong	textural
seductive	structured	tidy
sensational	stunning	timeless
sensual	sturdy	top-of-the-line
sentimental	stylish	tough
serene	suave	traditional
shamanic	sublime	tranquil
shapely	subtle	transcendent
sharp	succulent	treasured
silly	suitable	trendy

continued on next page

A long list of descriptive adjectives

CONTINUED FROM PREVIOUS PAGE

tropical	urban	welcoming
true	usable	whimsical
ugly	useful	wholesome
uncommon	valuable	wicked
uncomplicated	versatile	wild
unconventional	vibrant	witty
understated	visual	wonderful
unexpected	vital	woodsy
unique	vivacious	worldly
unparalleled	voluptuous	youthful
unrivaled	wanted	zany
unusual	warm	zesty
upscale	weird	

Words for intangible qualities

an air of	flourish	seemingly
ambience	fundamental	semblance
aspect	glamour	sensation
atmosphere	hint of	sense
attitude	impression	sensibility
aura	inherent	soul
characteristic	intrinsic	spirit
distillation	magic	style
elan	mojo	subtle
element	overtones	suggestion
energy	pizzazz	trace
essence	presence	twist
feeling	property	undertones
flair	reminiscent of	vibe

What Will It Do?

Action words

Positive words about what an item will do, or what it will do for you

accent	breathe	dance
accentuate	brighten	dare
accessorize	bring	dazzle
accommodate	buy	define
accomplish	capture	delight
add	carry	delineate
admire	celebrate	deliver
adorn	change	demonstrate
affirm	cherish	depict
aid	choose	develop
allow	collect	discover
amaze	comfort	display
appreciate	communicate	elevate
assist	compare	embellish
attract	complete	empower
balance	connect	enchant
bask	contain	encircle
beautify	contrast	energize
become	contribute	engage
beguile	cradle	enhance
benefit	create	enjoy
blend	crown	enrich
bless	cultivate	enthrall

continued on next page

Action words

CONTINUED FROM PREVIOUS PAGE

entice	indulge	refresh
evoke	inform	relax
exceed	intoxicate	relish
explore	invite	remind
express	juxtapose	replenish
feature	keep	reveal
fill	kiss	revel
fit	lead to	revitalize
fix	light	revive
flatter	love	rock
flow	luxuriate	satisfy
focus	match	seduce
frame	mix	serve
furnish	move	shape
further	nurture	shine
gain	perfect	show
gather	perform	show off
gratify	please	showcase
harmonize	pop	smile
help	preserve	snuggle
honor	protect	solve
illuminate	prove	soothe
illustrate	provide	spark
imagine	radiate	speaks
impress	reach	stimulate
improve	recall	streamline
include	reflect	strengthen

Action words

CONTINUED FROM PREVIOUS PAGE

succeed	sweeten	trust
suit	touch	update
surpass	transform	upgrade
surprise	transport	uplift
surround	treasure	value
sustain	treat	work

Phrases that describe benefits

a breath of fresh air

a conversation piece

a great pick-me-up

a nurturing gift

add a festive touch

add a new dimension

add a touch of beauty

add interest to a room

add some sparkle

at your fingertips

attention-getter

brighten your day

create a balance

create an atmosphere

create your look

enjoy it every day

everyone will notice

experience for yourself

express your love

express your style

feel the magic

feel young again

for that special someone

for the people you love

fun for the family

get many compliments

get more out of

give the best gift

good times

have fun

help the environment

instant gratification

join the party

just what you are looking for

make a huge difference

make a statement

make an impression

make it easy

makes all the difference

nothing else like it

pamper yourself

peace of mind

perfect for home or office

provide the finishing touch

relaxing and comfortable

save time

savor the moment

see for yourself

sets the stage

solve the problem

stay healthy

take control

wear it proudly

will last a lifetime

you deserve it

you will treasure

Phrases that describe benefits

CONTINUED FROM PREVIOUS PAGE

you'll be satisfied

your good taste

you'll fall in love with

your personal collection

you'll look great

you'll love it

continued on next page

How Was It Made?

Words that describe technique or craft

adaptation
aesthetic
affixed
altered
archival quality
artistry
assembled
built
composed
composite
constructed
craftsmanship
detailed
embellished
engineered
executed
fabricated
finely crafted
finished
forged
formed
form and function
hand crafted
hand-built
hand-carved
hand-cut
hand-decorated

hand-dyed
hand-engraved
hand-finished
handmade
hand-sculpted
hand-stitched
hand-tooled
handwoven
invented
layered
masterpiece
method
meticulous
modeled
molded
performed
precision
premium materials
produced
quality construction
reconstructed
reinforced
signature
welded
well built
work of art
workmanship

Words for recycled, upcycled, "green"

all natural	organic	rescued
biodegradable	post-consumer	restored
conscious	pure	retrofit
conservation	reclaimed	reuse
earth	recreated	reusable
earth-inspired	recycled	revived
eco-friendly	reduce	salvaged
ecological	refashioned	socially
ecosystem	refurbished	responsible
green	reinvented	sustainable
habitat	remodeled	upcycled
local	renewable	
natural	repurposed	

What Style Is It?

Art styles and design eras

See page 35, or use your internet search engine to find definitions and examples of these styles

Abstract Expressionism
Art Deco
Art Nouveau
Arts and Crafts
Bauhaus
Computer Age
Constructivism
Cubism
Dada
Edwardian
Edwardian Baroque
Expressionism
Fauvism
Folk Art
Futurism
Georgian
Gothic
High Victorian
Impressionism
International style
La Belle Époque

Mid Victorian
Midcentury Modern
Minimalism
Modernism
Neo Georgian
Neo vernacular
Neoclassicism
Op Art
Outsider Art
Photorealism
Pointillism
Pop Art
Post Impressionism
Post war brutalism
Postmodern classicism
Postmodernism
Realism
Romanticism
Surrealism
Symbolism
Victorian

More styles and subcultures

See next page, or use your internet search engine to find definitions and examples of these styles and subcultures

abstract	fetish	lolita
antique	folk	lowbrow
athletic	fusion	military
avant-garde	geekery	minimalist
bohemian	gladiator	mod
boho	glam	modern
boho chic	glam rock	natural
boho luxe	goth	nautical
bold	gothic	neo-classical
burlesque	gothic lolita	nerd
business	grunge	new age
constructed	headbanger	noir
costume	high fashion	nostalgic
cottage	hip hop	organic
cottage chic	hippie	patriotic
contemporary	hipster	prairie
country	historical	preppy
country western	Hollywood	primitive
cowboy	horror	psychedelic
cyberpunk	humorous	punk
deconstructionist	indie	rave
eclectic	industrial	realist
eco	jungle	regency
ethnic	kawaii	retro
fantasy	kitsch	rockabilly

More styles and subcultures

CONTINUED FROM PREVIOUS PAGE

rock and roll	surfer	waldorf
rocker	techie	weird
rustic	techno	whimsical
shabby	tiki	woodland
skater	traditional	zen
steampunk	tribal	
street style	vintage	

Some style categories defined

These terms are mostly quite subjective and open to many interpretations. These definitions introduce some possible concepts and interpretations; you should do your own research for any kind of in-depth understanding.

Abstract: Abstract art is nonrepresentational, not concrete, figurative, using illusion, imagery, often using lines, colors, and geometrical forms. It reflects the artist's interpretation as opposed to a realistic interpretation.

African: Traditional African art often includes emphasis on the human figure, is sculptural, more abstract than realistic; using natural materials such stone, beads, wood, textiles, etc. The term may also be used for animal prints and safari-style items.

Art Deco: A 1920s–30s style that influenced architecture, interior design, fashion, jewelry, and the visual arts. Decorative and ornamental, Art Deco uses stylized figures, straight, clean lines, symmetry, geometric designs, and a modern, sleek appearance. Motifs often include chevrons, fountains, and sunbursts.

continued on next page

Style Definitions, continued from previous page

Art Nouveau: Most popular around 1890–1910, strongly influenced by Czech artist Alphonse Mucha, the art nouveau style is full of flowing lines and curves, earthy colors, stylized women, and ornate flowers.

Asian: A very broad term that may include Chinese, Afghan, Japanese, Indian, Korean, Philippine, Indonesian, Vietnamese, Thai, Tibetan, and more. May also be applied to Buddhist imagery, feng shui symbols, chinese calligraphy, etc.

Athletic: Mostly a fashion term, this might include items that are sporty, sturdy, versatile and with clean lines. Might include sportswear or yoga style items.

Avant Garde: Using innovation, new concepts and techniques, experimental, cutting edge, ahead of its time, pushing the boundaries of what is accepted.

Bohemian: artistic, creative, unconventional, quirky, avant-garde, offbeat, edgy.

Boho: Items with Bohemian and hippie influences, colorful, floaty, peasant skirts, beads, fringe, wild patterns, ethnic styles, tie-dye and batik, etc. Variations include "Boho-chic" and "Boho-luxe".

Country Western: Cowboy, cowgirl, Western styles, boots, leather, hats, Southwestern U.S. influence.

Edwardian: Characteristic of the reign of Edward VII of Great Britain, which followed the Victorian era. In fashion these styles included slightly more comfortable corsets, high necklines, Gibson Girl style, wide-brim hats with feathers. Themes included high society, prosperity, and fashion finery. In jewelry, this period was characterized by delicate filigree in white gold and platinum, with diamonds and pearls predominating.

Fantasy: Magical, medieval, mythical, supernatural, fairytale, make-believe, otherworldly, myth and legend, often including images of wizards, witches, dragons, fairies, elves, and other creatures.

Folk: Folk Art typically refers to art created by people who lack formal art training, often regional art. It is frequently imaginative and simplistic, lacking in proportion and perspective, and using bold colors. It might include "primitive" styles. Many countries and cultures have their own versions of folk art.

Goth: Usually refers to a dark, sometimes morbid, eroticized fashion and style and usually involving a lot of black—black hair, dark clothing and pale complexions. Influenced by punk and Victorian styles, goth style might include materials such as black velvet, lace, fishnets, leather, corsets, gloves, stilettos and religious or occult themes. Motifs include skulls, crosses, etc. Goth has many subgenres with their own styles.

High Fashion: Haute couture, designer fashion, well-made and expensive, often exclusive or custom made.

Hip Hop: A style expression of Hip Hop culture, which is constantly evolving but frequently includes urban streetwear, sports jerseys, baggy pants, bright colors and strong graphics, heavy jewelry. Might include elements of skater fashion.

Hippie: Beads, fringe, wild patterns, ethnic styles, tie-dye and batik, peasant skirts, flowers, headbands, flowing colorful clothing, pendants, big glasses, macramé, lots of decoration.

Hipster: References a contemporary subculture that's a little hard to define but might include afficionados of urban culture, alternative rock, independent film, minimalist style, with geek or nerd elements, bicycles, tight pants, hats, mustaches, etc.

Historical: Items that relate to any specific time period in history, reflected accurately.

continued on next page

Style Definitions, continued from previous page

Hollywood Regency: 1930s "Hollywood Golden Age" glitz and glamour, over-the-top interior styles with expensive fabrics, sculptural textures, and a feeling of luxury and opulence.

Industrial: A design trend emphasizing sharp lines, salvaged items, metals, heavy woods, factory items, heavy but sophisticated pieces.

Kawaii: A Japanese fashion term meaning cute, lovable, or adorable. Originally aimed at girls or teenagers but has now expanded to a larger market., might include animé and manga, cute mascot characters, candy or pastel colors, baby animals, etc.

Kitsch: Tacky or campy, frequently describing something that is overly sentimental, melodramatic, or gaudy. Originally a derogatory term but now often used in a positive way to describe things from popular culture eras or events.

Mediterranean: Sunny, natural, nautical, earthy vibrant colors, romantic but casual, water features, somewhat rustic. Colors might include azure blue, white, terracotta.

Mid-Century: An architectural, interior, and product design form from the mid-20th century involving clean lines and organic simplicity, and often with curvy geometric shapes. Scandinavian industrial design is an influence. Related terms might include mod, retro, atomic age, "mid-mod", 1950s.

Military: Self-explanatory style with grays, khaki greens and browns, brass buttons, lace-up boots, items that are functional, understated, heavily tailored, with sharp forms.

Minimalist: Modern style with straight lines, simple geometric shapes, smooth textures, functional design with limited visual elements. Anything stripped to it's bare essentials.

Mod: Early 1960s London subculture with later revivals with a smooth, sophisticated look that emphasized tailor-made suits, mohair clothes, thin ties, button-down collars, jumpers, pointed-toe shoes, mini-skirts, go-go boots, geometric shapes, and sharp cuts. The term is also sometimes used to describe anything that is believed to be popular, fashionable, or modern.

Modern: A style represented by clean, straight lines, stainless steel, chrome and other metals, minimalist design, simplicity, bright bold colors.

Nautical: Apparel or decor related to the ocean, boating, the beach, or a coastal lifestlye. Colors include blue, white, red, black, stripes. Nautical fashion is about preppy, tailored shapes. Motifs include anchors, captain's wheels, boats, shells, grommets, ropes and tassels, lighthouses, marine animals, stars, mermaids.

Neo-classical: A style that draws inspiration from the classical art and culture of Ancient Greece or Ancient Rome, but with a modern twist.

Preppy: Originally used in relation to Northeastern private university preparatory schools—dress, mannerisms, and etiquette reflecting Ivy League, upper-class families in the United States. Examples include blazers, argyle sweaters, chinos, madras, button down Oxford shirts, and boat shoes or loafers, checks and plaid patterns.

Primitive: A style of rustic simplicity—folk art, country farmhouse decor that has a feeling of warmth and simplicity. Solid rustic furniture, pantry boxes, baskets, crocks, rugs, linens, peg racks, rusty metal objects.

Regency: In architecture or furniture, Regency is related to neoclassical style, but with forms made heavier, larger and more ornamental, often with an element of the exotic—Turkish, Indian and Egyptian. In clothing a Jane Austen-type look, empire silhouettes, flowing skirts, sheer muslin, bonnets, soft colors.

continued on next page

Style Definitions, continued from previous page

Renaissance: Renaissance clothing refers to clothes in a wide range of styles, colors, and materials as worn across Europe from the mid-1300s through the 1500s. The term may refer to Renaissance Fair medieval style clothing: corsets, codpieces, underskirts, bodices, hoops, berets, square-cut collars, rich brocades and velvets, etc.

Resort: Resort wear, also Cruise wear, originally referring to upscale stores selling to affluent customers who spend the winter in warm climates. Now Resort might mean a specialized clothing style including Hawaiian shirts, walking shorts, caftans, sandals, casual, yet fashionable clothing made from cotton, silk, microfiber, poplin—that are easy to pack, lightweight and breathable, frequently including nautical or floral designs.

Retro: Usually referring to design styles from the 1950s, 60s, and 70s, but the term now can mean almost anything even slightly vintage. The actual item may not be old, but might reference styles of the past.

Rocker: Originally referring to British biker subculture, this style might now include heavily-decorated leather motorcycle jackets, metal studs, leather, tall boots, band shirts, jumpsuits, punky rebel or tattoo apparel of many kinds.

Rustic: Rough-hewn, simply made, using sturdy, wood, metal, earthy colors. Rural, unsophisticated, with country charm.

Sci-Fi: High-tech, post-industrial, retro-futuristic. In fashion this might mean one-piece,
skin-tight, shiny metal, plastic boots, latex. Motifs include spaceships, robots, and aliens. Items might also be derived from science fiction characters in books or movies.

Shabby: "Shabby cottage" or "cottage chic". Items usually have a soft, feminine feel with a distressed antique look. Furniture may be heavily painted in off-whites or pastels. Vintage linens, chenille, lace and roses.

Southwestern: A tribute to the American southwest, this style often includes earth-tone colors, rough textures, handcrafted objects, brightly colored woven fabrics, adobe or terra cotta, Native American designs, desert colors, wood, leather, pottery and stone.

Spooky: Halloween style, scary but cute. Haunted houses, ghosts, witches, spiders, etc., black and orange.

Steampunk: Victorian meets modern, technology meets romance, with a dose of science fiction and fantasy. A combination of modern styles influenced by the Victorian era, Steampunk may be characterized by earthy colors and jewel tones, opulent design, Victorian lines, and may include items of a mechanical nature clockwork, boiler rivets, old keys or some kind of industrial objects. Fashion items include gowns, corsets, petticoats, bustles, boots, suits with vests, coats, top hats, goggles, and many eclectic pieces.

Techie: Related to computers or electronics, also Geekery.

Traditional: In furniture Georgian, Victorial, Colonial, with elegant design, grand and stately. Or this term may just mean anything that is done in a well established and time honored way.

Tribal: Pertaining to the visual arts and culture of indigenous peoples, items in this style frequently include natural materials, wood, beads, feathers, stone, figurative design and geometric shapes.

Victorian: Refers to the Victorian era, or the reign of Queen Victoria (1837–1901). The style is highly ornamented, extravagant, romantic, luxurious, with curvy lines, dark rich colors or soft pastels, lace, velvet, fringes and tassels, cameos. Fashion is characterized by tight corsets, gigantic hoop-skirts, and outrageous bustles, while furniture is heavy and highly stylized.

continued on next page

Style Definitions, continued from previous page

Woodland: Influenced by nature, with earth tones, natural materials, botanical designs and forest animal motifs, usually presented in a sweet or cute style.

Zen: This style is about balance and simplicity, calm and peaceful design, Japanese influence, meditation and serenity. Home decor might include minimal furniture, plants, bamboo, water features, linen screens, a tranquil minimalist space.

Words that describe era or time period

PAST

age-old
ageless
anachronistic
ancestral
antiquated
antique
authentic
bygone
classic
collectible
enduring
eternal
hearkens back
heirloom
heritage
historical
immortal
inheritance
keepsake
lasting
legacy
legendary
memento
memorabilia
memorial
nostalgic
old school
old world
origins
pays homage to
prehistoric
quaint
rare
relic
retro
retro-futuristic
roots
storied
test of time
timeless
traditional
treasure
vintage
weathered
yesteryear

PRESENT/ FUTURE

avant garde
contemporary
current
cutting edge
futuristic
in vogue
latest
modern
new
postmodern
recent
trendy
uber-modern
ultramodern
up-to-date

Who Is It For?

Words that describe audience or market

active
adults
animal lover
artists
babies
bikers
bloggers
boomers
boss
boyfriend
boys
brother
businessperson
cats
child
children
collectors
cooks
coworker
crafter
decorator
dogs
eccentric
educated
engineer

environmentalist
do-it-yourselfer
fashionista
father
fiancé
foodie
friends
gag gift
gardeners
geek
girlfriend
girls
grandmother
grandfather
guest
healthy
high tech
home business
home school
infants
kids
librarian
lovers
man cave
men

mentor
mother
movie lover
music lover
nature lover
nerd
older
pets
political
readers
rebel
relatives
religious
retired
rural
school
secretary
senior
shopper
sister
social
sports enthusiast
staff
students
style-conscious

continued on next page

Words that describe audience or market

CONTINUED FROM PREVIOUS PAGE

successful	teens	vintage lovers
teachers	toddlers	women
team	traveler	writer
techie	urban	young

What Event Is It For?

List of events

anniversary	dance	open house
awards ceremony	dinner party	party
bachelor party	engagement	performance
bachelorette	festival	picnic
party	fiesta	pool party
baby shower	fundraiser	reception
bar mitzvah	game	retirement party
bat mitzvah	going away party	retreat
barbecue	graduation	reunion
birthday	grand opening	tailgate party
block party	holiday party	thank you
ceremony	luau	theme party
cocktail party	housewarming	tournament
competition	media event	wedding
concert	meet and greet	wedding shower
convention/	meeting	
trade show	memorial	
costume party	networking event	

Seasonal themes

Winter

basketball
beach vacations
entertaining
holidays
food and recipes
nesting
snow
winter sports

Spring

baseball
fresh, bright colors
gardening
home repair, DIY
spring cleaning
weddings

Summer

beach & swimming
cookouts
picnics
travel & vacation

Autumn

back-to-school
football season
harvest
leaves
warm, rich colors

List of holidays and seasonal events

A mostly-U.S. list, with apologies to others

January
New Years Day
Martin Luther King, Jr., Day
Chinese/Lunar New Year
Australia Day
Australian Open

February
National Freedom Day
Groundhog Day
Super Bowl Sunday
Presidents Day
Valentine's Day
Mardi Gras
Academy Awards
Grammy Awards
Washington's Birthday
Ash Wednesday
Black History Month

March
International Women's Day
St. Patrick's Day
Spring Equinox
Purim
National Women's History
    Month, U.S.

April
April Fool's Day
Jewish Passover Starts
Tax Day, US
Easter
Earth Day
Admin. Assistant's Day
Arbor Day
Prom

May
May Day
Cinco de Mayo
Cannes Film Festival
Bike to Work Day
Kentucky Derby
National Teacher Day
Nurses Day
Mother's Day
Armed Forces Day
Victoria Day, Canada
Memorial Day, U.S

June
Graduation
Flag Day
Father's Day
Juneteenth
Summer Solstice

continued on next page

List of holidays and seasonal events
CONTINUED FROM PREVIOUS PAGE

July
Canada Day, Canada
Independence Day, U.S
Tour de France
Bastille Day
Parent's Day

August
Friendship Day
Ramadan

September
Labor Day, U.S
Labour Day, Canada
Grandparent's Day
Rosh Hashanah
Fall Equinox
Yom Kippur
Native American Day
Oktoberfest
Talk Like a Pirate Day

October
National Day, China
Columbus Day, U.S
Thanksgiving, Canada
Boss Day
Halloween
Breast Cancer Awareness
Month

November
All Saints Day
All Souls Day
Dia de los Muertos (Day of
the Dead)
Election Day, U.S
Children's Day
Black Friday, Cyber Monday
Guy Fawkes Day, UK
Veterans Day, U.S
Remembrance Day (Alberta)
Thanksgiving Day, U.S

December
Start of Summer, Southern
Hemisphere
Hanukkah
Winter Solstice
Christmas Day
Boxing Day, Canada
Kwanzaa
New Year's Eve